A Dusting of Star Fall:
Love Poems

Sal Amico M. Buttaci

Some of these poems first appeared in the following publications:

Black Creek Review;
Poetic Page Opus;
Poetidings;
Poetry Exchange;
PoetryMagazine.com;
Promising the Moon;
Rattlesnake Review;
Steel Point Quarterly;
The Dusty Owl Quarterly;
Two Can Play This Game;
2 River View;
Voices;
White Line Productions, Inc.;
Writer's Club Webzine

A Dusting of Star Fall:
Love Poems

Sal Amico M. Buttaci

Cyberwit.net

4/2 B, L.I.G

Govindpur Colony,

Allahabad-211004 (U.P.)

India

Tel: (91) 09415091004

E-mail: cyberwit@rediffmail.com

www.cyberwit.net

Copyright © 2006 Sal Amico M. Buttaci

ISBN 81-8253-054-7

First Edition: 2006

Typeset by Vaishnavi Processors, Kamla Nagar, Allahabad

Printed in India at Astha Associates, D. N. Marg, Allahabad

Dedicated
to
Sharon:
wife, lover, soul mate,
friend

INTRODUCTION

In *A Dusting of Star Fall: Love Poems*, Sal Amico M. Buttaci, teacher, instructor, writer, and poet, has given us a gift to cherish. These poems, written for the poet's wife Sharon, contain a message for all of us in describing the fulfillment of a very human yearning—the desire to express love, to cherish the beloved, and, in return, to be cherished.

In one poem, "A Winter Walk," the poet captures a fleeting moment of memory preserved like a symbol of separation, however momentary. In another poem, "The Way You Looked at Me," he uses as a metaphor for love the image of a ship on its voyage to an earthly paradise and begs his love to take him there.

Sal Buttaci's poems are written for his wife, but they are, in a sense, written for all of us. In his poem, "On Display," he writes: "how love/ when nurtured/ can long survive."

He writes of love as the source of strength that sustains us through the trials and difficulties that sometimes befall us humans, and he reminds us also, in "Lost at Sea," just "what loveless means."

With the wisdom of a long-time teacher, this poet urges us in his poems to find and keep that one essential quality: the giving and sharing of love that can accompany us through life and render us partners in a sublime world of our own making.

Sal Buttaci is the author of several books, including *A Family of Sicilians: Stories and Poems* that contains some of his poems written in Sicilian and translated into English for our enjoyment. The book's poems and stories bring before us the essence of Sicilian life with all its humor, warmth, and friendship. Another book by Buttaci, *Promising the Moon*, was his first book of love poems to Sharon.

In his busy life the poet teaches English at Thomas Jefferson Middle School in Garfield, New Jersey, and writing courses as an adjunct professor at Bergen Community College in Paramus, New Jersey. His poems, stories, and letters have appeared in a variety of publications here and abroad, including *The New York Times, U.S.A. Today,* and *Christian Science Monitor.*

Sal Buttaci is an executive board member of the New Jersey Poetry Society, Inc., for which he recently gave a workshop on narrative poetry at the Princeton University Book Store in Princeton, New Jersey.

We can look forward to more poetic gems from this New Jersey poet. The love poems in this delightful book speak to our inmost feelings, and for that, his readers will be exceedingly thankful.

Moira Bailis
New Jersey poet and radio host

FROM THE AUTHOR

This poetry collection of mine has been nearly ten years in the writing. I began when I first met my wife back in August of 1996. I jotted poems down in small pocket pads, notebooks, and computer files. I submitted many of them to editors in hope of publication and delighted when they were accepted. It was an ideal way to share the feelings I had for Sharon with, hopefully, a great deal of readers. Sometime later I started filling small journals with poems and giving them to my wife on the occasions of her birthday, our anniversary, Easter, and Christmas. We would go out to dinner, then come home and I would read to her another book of poems.

Finally, putting these "Sharon" poems together in *A Dusting of Star Fall: Love Poems* made sense to me. Of all the poems I have written since the 1950s when I first began writing poems, this collection includes my favorites because they are all love-inspired. These poems that speak of my love for Sharon afford me the pleasant opportunity of delivering them from the deepest part of me into the light of written words so you can read them in this book. These poems express my belief that the love Sharon and I share truly does conquer all.

Sal Amico M. Buttaci
Lodi, New Jersey

CONTENTS

Which Hand

In my left a star
in my right
a beating heart
when I shuffle
from one hand
to the other

the star pulsates
where the heart was beating
and the heart sparkles
where the star had shone

I ask you to choose
the heart
the star
which hand
which hand

you say first the left
and then the right
but when I open each palm
in turn we are both amazed
to find only heart prints
in a fine dusting of star fall

Our House of Love

The slum lords
of poorly built
houses of love
envy the two of us.

Their eyes light up
piercingly green
when they see the castle
we have constructed

with the mortar and stone
of "I do" upon which,
story by story,
we take our place of love

skyward until one day
we will add
a golden steeple
where we will stand

tip-toed together
reaching up
to catch a cloud
to heaven.

Ritual

Two parties ceremoniously
commit their lives to each other
while the choir sings hymns
and loved ones sigh
or joyously sob.

Two parties courageously
sacrifice on the altar
a lamb or wild beast
to symbolize
the old death's self.

Two parties timidly
repeat the magic words,
then kiss in conformity
to love's rituals.

But I say beyond vows
and loving gestures,
beyond ritual and rite,
I will love you
beyond tradition
and convention,

for as long
as beats the rhythm
of time, until this heart
gives itself away
to the ritual
of life's final silence.

How the Two of Us

you say love is a hammer
pounding moments red-hot
on the anvil of time

a whisper you say
fluttering fragile and thin
as the breath of small birds

a rocket transporting us
to an absence of gravity
where truth is a lightheartedness

but I say love
is the way you·look at me
the tilt of your face
in the crook of my nighttime arm

or love is how the two of us
go on cheating death forever

On Display

I've saved all the moments
in this shadowbox of love

placed mementos under glass
so that passersby could stop

and study how love
when nurtured
can long survive.

On the Loose Again

Berserkers savagely mad
are out scouring the city streets
in search of true lovers
to brutalize and leave for dead.

What strange quarry to hunt and kill!
Why not politicians who lie?
Or how about terrorists?
Go hunt them down and leave us free!

Could it be jealousy?
I have watched those raving madmen
question all that's good and fair,
and rail against those who love life.

We have become their enemy.
Still, we must boldly proclaim our love,
shout it to the whole world
that we will not deny true love.

Berserkers may instill fear
in lovers who question themselves,
but as for us, let them bring it on!
We will bravely go on loving.

Lost at Sea

one day I found myself
lost in a sea of missing days
rowing nowhere
awestruck by the slosh
of foreign waters
and a darkening gray ceiling
of sky that appeared
to be crashing down on me

this is what loveless means
this is what the heart feels
in lonely places
this is the reason tears
flow from the well of
painful memories
why minds creak
past laughter
in familiar rooms

then you found me
lost on that tumultuous sea
waving my oar skyward
crying for deliverance

you suddenly appeared
an angel wingless
heart full of grace
wordless without guile
the restoration sculptor
of a heart
tarnished by false love's
deceit

The Way You Looked at Me

Once I swore I was invincible,
Stronger than water and fire,
But the way you looked at me,
The way you took my hand
That trembled like a new born
The smile you wore much brighter
Than my yellow fear
Convinced me love was a ship
Sailing for an earthly Paradise
And that I wanted more than life itself
For you to take me there.

Angels Dance

On the head of a pin
Angels dance to prove
We don't need much space
In this little life of ours
To prove God exists.

You say who you are;
I say who I am
And in the saying
We see how kindly
God makes Himself known.

Then we tell the world
One rhythmic step at a time
In one long dance
How both of us
Are at the same time

One
and
Two.

Falling in Love

In the spark of forgotten fire
a memory ignited me awake
and I caught myself dangling
from a high window of
a sad morning before all of me
separated from the sill.

Before I could plummet
to a hard pavement death
you saved me with
a loving hand
and I held on,
falling on this side of the window

into the saving arms
of your heroic love.

Writing Poems

All over the world
Fools like me
Are writing poems
Of love and joy
Of sorrow and loneliness

They are called poets
These fools like me
Hunched over pens
And computer screens
Getting words down

Retrieved from files
Deep in the brain
Arranged in bins
Filled with things
To say
By fools like me

It is happening
Everywhere
Millions of
Poem players
Word hunters
Rhyme jugglers
Fools like me.

Outside War, West Virginia

Along Berwind Lake the stretching pines
reflect themselves on a surface of concentric
circles where paddling ducks disturb
the winnows in their underwater
wrigglings. Marveling at nature we
say how all of this will go on.

Without words in this natural place
you and I watch quiet pines poke a
blue sky, and we swear in the twinkling
of our eyes that we too will go on
forever: our love vibrant and green-eternal.

Berwind Lake

When the West Virginia sun awakens,
lifts the brightest head from dawn's dark pillow,
and reveals her golden face behind the hills,
it's then that day takes its cue and lights up
Berwind Lake, dazzling all the pine trees there.

Dragonflies zigzag their wings in fancy flights
above the tranquil waters of the lake,
while birds ruffle free from arbored sleep
and sail across the blue and green divide.

Flowers bow to the flitter of hummingbirds.
To witness this delightful morning dawn
is to proclaim God's power and His love.
How wonderful a God Who re-creates
Berwind Lake each day out of darkness!

On this summer morning the breeze is God's breath.
And what of us? The way two lovers
return each summer and walk that wooden bridge,
then sit, shaded at a picnic table,
to reminisce about our nine good years
together while we marvel at the long
green line of proud trees along the edge of
Berwind Lake.

Berwind Lake Revisited

If I could, I would name all of these flowers,
Say which trees end before tall times begin,
What starts the ducks to quack on Berwind Lake,
Be privy to the secrets insects tell,
And ride within an empty cellophane bag
That sails its crinkled shape upon the lake.

Today, like last year, and again the year before,
We sat here at our familiar picnic
Place of stone and wood,
Witnesses to a West Virginia June
Where nature plays out its green again,
And the bridge, like a wooden rainbow,

Spans the lake between the roadside and the wild.
Here we are once more— the two of us
Still locked in life's embrace— same time, same place,
Our love like seasons renewed, yet changeless
Like this summer scene on Berwind Lake.

Berwind Lake: August 25, 2005

I spied a mallard duck on Berwind Lake
and watched it dunk its head beneath
the water top, then glide as if on ice
across the surface of the lake.

How peaceful is this August scene!
Pine trees stretch long green branches
into gray shadows resting blurrily
upside-down under the water

While an alchemist sun transforms ripples
into a floating jeweler's cloth
of sparkling diamonds.
Who are we to disturb nature's tranquility!

The biting flies, the pesky gnats,
even that duck sunning wet wings on
the jutting rock in the center of the lake,
remind us of our intrusion.

We come here to relive an annual August
ritual—you with camera, I with poet's pen—
then as we head uphill towards our Toyota
for the winding ride to Yukon,

I cannot help but realize our nine years
together is a mere raindrop in this
picture-postcard scene of our ageless
Berwind Lake.

A Lesson in Humility

Bugs hardly visible
to the naked eye
fly fearlessly
to naked flesh
on those evening porch nights
in Yukon, West Virginia,
that leave this man (a grown man),
a man who prides himself
a man in control,
this man in love with you,
scratching uncontrollably,
tearing skin deep enough
to look a bloody fool,
scratching arms and legs
and neck and hands
and face and chest—
a slap-happy lunatic
without any pride at all.

You Can Tell Them
You Are 39

We can move away to a hut
in the Himalayas,
to a boat house on the Ganges,
somewhere two strangers
to the world,
and you can tell them
you are 39,
that it'll be a long time
before you are 50.

You can say how happy
39 makes you feel,
then before the year is gone,
we can once again move on
to some far-away tribe
in the rain forests
or the jungle
or a space station near the moon

and you can tell them
you are 39,
how 50's far away.
You can sing the praises of 39,
and then just before
September 4th
we can move away again,
set up a house of bamboo
and thatched roof
somewhere along

China's Yellow River.
Tell them all you're 39.
You're 39, a long way to 50.
Tell them all
you are 39.

Anagrams of
"Two in Love"

NOW
on the
VINE
of our
VOW
we
VIEW
all we have left to
WIN.
each
LINE
of these poems
WENT
into a lover's
TIN,
LIVE
with our memories:
They
WON'T
ever fade.

Everything I've Rehearsed a Lifetime

If I could just this once declare my love,
Say this or that about the one who gives
This heart of mine riches to be proud of,
One time at least say exactly what lives
Within my deepest self where no one goes,
Oh, I would sprinkle words on angel's wings,

Bid kudos to the sky—farewell to woes!
See feeble words grow strong, say everything
I've rehearsed a lifetime of days and nights,
And watch them soar to the gates of Heaven
To be blessed, then to Sharon words take flight.
For each true word I give, she'll give seven.

Before this voice of mine in time grows mute,
I pray I find the words to speak love's truth.

I Mourned Like Job

If I had chosen then to question how
The impatient man in time can reap rewards,
Today I'd still be lonely as a cloud.
Those painful years when sorrow's cruel allure
Would tempt me to the edge of losing faith
In all good love that matters in this life.

But I kept strong and swore that I would wait
For God in His good time to send a wife.
How strange those years that seemed to never end!
I mourned like Job the loss of what I owned,
But then somehow the Lord sent Sharon, friend
And wife: the dearest soul I've ever known.

So this to all whose hearts are filled with pain:
Be patient: God can make you whole again.

If Chasing Love

If chasing love were worth one's precious time,
most everyone would spend their days and nights
concocting potions, setting traps, and such
to win the hearts of those they deem sublime
and they would find it all within their right
to chain these hearts and love them very much.

But I have come to know it's not the way,
for love is not a quarry to be hunted down,
a beast to chase and then chain as one's one.
Love's more than that; it's more than I can say.
Love seeks out those where love's already found;
it frees two lovers from being alone.

Together we will face the years ahead
and keep love strong as when we first had wed.

To Love and Be Loved

The heart
consents
to love;
the brain,
to be loved.
The magic rests
in the marriage
of the two.

The Irony of Love

We dive into the fires
Convinced
We won't be burned,
Yet love
Demands
The flames
Consume us.

September 4, 1955

If I could have known
That Sunday before
The first day
Of my 8th grade
You were being
Born at about 10:30 A.M.
Somewhere in War, WV,
I would have better enjoyed
That last day of
Summer freedom.

In the Folds of Angels' Wings

All our dreams in the safeguard of
Angels who protect them!
Do what you will, world, but you will
Not divide us. Time, you will
Wear us down but never apart.
Wings of angels shelter us from storms
And we thrive in the folds of their
Robes. Cover us, Angels, with comforters
Of soft down. Turn dark clouds into
White so the sun will always shine through.

Count Gilu Motel

Art appreciation came to the Count Gilu,
etched forever in memory. Your reflection
in the mirror. Each of us holding
the stare that pinned us eye to
eye, two floating souls in a frame
of suspended time. What did we see in
the mirror's confession? That you are
beholder to me; that I am beholder to you.

Magic Markers

Angels filled the spaces we left bare,
fanning out inside the room.
Wings like plumes of giant birds,
arrows free of quiver, soft-tipped, Gabriel's
horn blaring soundlessly like
magic to our ears. We took
markers and flaired the Sharon-Sal
naming of each other, paintings of
us in near-abstractions. Then in the
waters warm as August, we stooped to
washing away free-hand body art
out from the tingling pores of our skin.
Color beads cascaded in rivulets
on to the soapy surface of bathwater.
That scene can never be forgotten: that
night saved forever in secret hiding places.

Moments in First-Time

Viewing pictures in my mind of then, a
video of those mid-August nights we spent,
movies of our beginning time... Oh, how
we enjoyed ourselves with simple things!
How we both laughed in each other's company,
wanting to be nowhere else! We ate at Pizza Hut
one night. Bags of candy on the dresser.
Remember the sandwiches we made, then tipsy in
a kaleidoscopic spin we wine-toasted each other
in the name of forever during those moments
in First-Time when no one could have been cooler
than we were? No one.

Time's Passing

there is something sad
about the ending
of another year.
Each one seems
to pass behind our backs
while life distracts us.

We try but fail
to hold each one
in our embrace,
then watch the year
tumble its number
into Time's fire.

What Love Is Not

Candy heavy in chocolate
to die for, flowers that pleasure
the eye, then too soon wilt and die,

These are perishable symbols
of what love is.

Words Cannot Say

Gifts from a speechless man,
an empty-handed wanderer,
a soul whose intentions
you could look through
like flimsy butterfly wings
and know somehow
sometimes words cannot say
the inside of a man.

When Love Is Gone

Pale and thin
a shiny wisp
of leaf sailing
in an autumn air—
Is this what
the absence of love is?

Don't Say How I Should Know

Don't ask me to define
these feelings I knead
like bread till they rise
so high I cannot contain them.
Don't say how I should know
enough by now
to slice the heart
and serve love
with words
clear as teardrops.

Winter Walk

A wave of the hand
and I leave you
on your alley walk
sidestepping patches
of stubborn snow
and ice black
as night
and I wonder
if you memorized
that scene
as I have saved mine
in my memory.

Even When Darts Pierced Me

When Cupid aimed his dart
at me, I cowered,
hid from his assault,
because I feared
the wounds of love.
Then I met you
and even when darts
pierced this heart
red and bleeding,
I sought no ointment,
no salve to save me
from the scars of love.

Snow Still Falls

Snow still falls
as when loveless
I lived my days
a prisoner
talking to cell walls.

The snow still falls,
moments trickle away,
day raises its
sunny head,
a dab of white moon

splotches night
that darkens all,

but now I have you.

Avoiding Terrors of the Heart

What difference
does it make
if we remain at war
or Osama
sends his suicide soldiers
crashing through
our basement window
or Saddam goes free
to breathe
toxic breath on Lodi!
As long as my hand
clasps your hand,
we are at peace.

Call the "Thought" Police!

Tell them in no uncertain terms
how I emptied my head
of life's heartaches,
rendered it empty
as a dry well,
then filled it
to the brim of brain with
only thoughts of you
and me, fly swatters
in our hands, killing
the pesky bugs of those
thoughts distracting us
from us.

Like Voyagers

I knew when I met you
time would pass
and we with it
like voyagers on a sea
of days and years.
Somehow I knew
loneliness would fly
high above us,
a giant vulture
cawing to our deaf ears;
I knew the waters
would be calm,
hypnotic,
smooth as love.

Thunder in the Hollow

Remember the West Virginia summer
thunder rattled through the hollow,
shaking us from stone-cradled dreams?
Up there in the mountain darkness
Spears of lightening split our sleepy
faces, open-eyed now, in a jagged
symmetry of black and white.
What had we been dreaming when
the thunder boomed? Comfortable
in the depths of sleep, we walked which
familiar unknown streets? What fabrications
in that dream world did we so readily
accept? And thunder, rousting us
from the cocoon of sleep, what did
it signify? Perhaps that life and love
and truth go on outside the trappings
of safe summer dreaming.

Promising the Moon Again

A wise man once said
Love is eternal
and for love's sake
true lovers would give away
all things—
breath as well.
Once I promised you
the moon
but still he hangs
like a bright ornament
in the dark skies.
One night when he's asleep,
I shall steal him, bag him,
and bring him to your arms.

Driving on a Sunday Afternoon

Peripherally I welcome into my vision
A feast of yellow crocuses, red anemones,
Waving fields of red tulips and wild gladioli.

Then you ask me why I hold my tongue
When Mother Nature speaks,
Why I delight to feel her warm whispers
At my cheek.

A Walk Along Sandy Hook Beach (July 1997)

You tap the wood in whose crevices
History imbedded itself
And you call it "something from the sea,"
A twisted relic of what grew once

Along the prehistoric trunk line
Of green parasols, eons before
This grittiness lay here, golden gems—
Silicone grains that once formed mountains

Long before humanity came, armed
With names for seasons, names for all things,
As if that would insure survival.

You tap this wood from a tree that fell
Crashing though unheard by witnesses,
Wood adrift in time like horns
From a slaughtered bull, or gnarled fingers
Pointing somewhere before all this.

Love's Design

A
heart
is
one
symmetrical
drawing
of
two
curves
meeting
at
the
center
locked
in
a
heartbeat.

Bubble

Hermetically sealed,
protected from
the whoosh of traffic
outside us,
we call our love
"air" and "sustenance";
we marvel at life
spoiling outside
our bubble.
This is the flower
of love's reward:
time cannot wilt
what flutters
inside us.

September

When the last of summer treads her bare feet
away from sandy beaches, the ocean
is left solely to the creatures of the water,
and autumn hovers in the cyclic wings,
waiting to be born again.

It has been this way since time's first breath.
A caped September glides in long brisk strides.
He waves his fall wand and suddenly
the leaves of blanched green tumble soundlessly
From the outstretched limbs of oaks and elms.

Is

The wise have held discourse
on matters open to debate.
They pontificate, defending points
sometimes untouched for centuries.
They claim they've looked to the heavens
with eyes squinting through the glass
of the astronomer and found causes
for the universe in the bellies
of holes black as the blind can see.
But never have the wise dared analyze
Love in all its myriad transformations,
never once said beyond
the inexplicable:
"Love simply is."

The Month

The twelve timekeepers march
down their days to the dictates
of seasonal demands
whether in snow or rain
or under the hottest of suns.
Each one is a troop of days
landing their heavy boots
in a synchronized rhythm
of passing time. Each month's
a soldier playing out destiny
year after year, then disappears
until called again to its proper turn.
Compassionate, but cool
and resolute, September knows
it cannot revive a dying August.

Star Fall

inside the world
of a single
snowflake
we tumble
through our lives

the points
of our star
falling like daggers
in the wind

still we vow
to face with gallantry
our quick descent into
meltdown

For Spite Winter Kills

Relentless winter
decolorizes
everything.

It squeezes hues
and shades from
shapes and forms.

It freezes the song
trembling birds sing
to the cold air.

It disarms surviving
wasps and hornets
of their stings.

It weighs down
the traveling-south
bird's wing.

It chills the living
to the bone
with blizzard storms.

Winter decrees
the world be
sparkling white,

freezing out
all signs of green
for spite.

Red and Green Poems

red and green poems
dazzle us now
in their abandon

their words sparkle
and dance through lines
in perfect time

they amaze us
and we tremble
to find ourselves

we dive beneath
the surface
of the red and green

to discover
the words down there
define our lives

and if we could
we'd never swim
to the surface

we'd lose ourselves
to the motion
of the stanzas

we'd live out our days
in green and red;
we'd let the words

say who we are
and believe them.

City of Ice

Love is the sun
Melting a city of ice.
The magic wand
Of the good wizard,
The luck charm
Around the neck of Time.

Love is the hero
Who saves lives
Perilously tottering
On the edge.

Love is a painter
Of smiles.

Halloween Make-Over

The yellow moon
envies the orange
pumpkin
in a field of vines.
He floats in a dark
Halloween sky
streaked with
witches on brooms.

The moon would like
just this one night
to be orange,
to mix into his
yellow pastiness
enough blood
to turn him
orange.
He would like
just this one evening

to peel away
sickly pale skin,
trade in craters
for pumpkin creases,
wear a green-stem hat,
conceal himself
in hideaway vines,
conceal his moonness
from the brandished
blade of some child's

father.

The moon would like
this All Hallows Eve
to let go the tides,
vacate a star-studded
sky, and slip
plummeting
like a stone
through God's
fingers.

Spells

If spells could
Rightly be cast
Or potions
Taken on the tongue
Could make dreams
Come true,

I would network
Among the witches
And the wizards
For this alone:

A long life
To love you
Magically
Forever.

If Only I Could

If I could stitch the fabric of these threading years
until to the touch no seam could betray
where one year ended, the next began;

If I could pitch the pennies of the luckless hours
into a well deeper than wayward thoughts
and save the treasure for an even bleaker day;

If I could wish for elusive dreams to lay themselves
before my hands like the tamed before the conqueror
and witness how these dreams transform my life;

If I could ditch all self-destructing fears that paralyze
hope and leave me stranded on the highway
of a life trafficked beyond what one should endure;

If I could hitch my wagon to a star, place all my trust
in God, say, "Take these worries from me,"
and then love God with all my heart and soul;

If I could do all this, what wonders this world
would open up to me! Good health, love and laughter
would be my entourage as I walk with you

down the sunny roads of my remaining days.

Dream City

I saw you in a dream city
where the sun
played its rays
on yellow daffodils
and you held
the reddest rose.

You were selling
velvet petals
in a flower fair
filled with children
and they all loved you,
their faces beaming.

I called your name,
letters softly whispering
from my lips,
but you did not
acknowledge me.

Then the flowers
came alive
and danced
with the children
as I floated
towards you.
The sun
grew hot enough
to melt the two of us,
transforming us

into human rivers
flowing down
a red/blue/orange
street of fire.

What the Sky Says

It does not speak: The spirit
of those high blue skies.
It floats silently
on the dazzling
floor of Heaven.

It dances through silly-putty clouds
and wherever its steps go,
wonders appear: angels and rabbits
and faces all smiling, a stampede
of wild beasts kicking up dust
in a white shower of sky.

The spirit of blue has nothing to speak.
Whatever it's thinking can never be known.
It's alone in its heaven, skipping down
white formations of what objects
you see. It's all up to the spirit
what objects you see as it slides
under clouds and snuggles

beneath blankets of blue
as it glides without speaking,
without saying a word.
Look! Now a forest of white trees,
now a highway of gray.

Unfair

Again,
with the fall
of day,
we saw
how unfair
life is.

An opossum
lay in a mangle
of blood.

Somewhere
a dog barked,
a cat screeched,
someone behind
a window wept.

Darkness fell
in a sudden heap
of undone
things.

Purple

Unrhymable,
friendless
in a world
of color,
you cloak
the king,
the eggplant,
and sometimes
splash across
the late-day
sky to mystify
lovers of
all ages and
color

It's Your Call

You could set on fire
all the heartbeats
I have left,
blow away
the breaths
I am saving
for my old age

if you wanted.

You could squeeze
blood from this
stone, crumble
the mountain
of me to powder,
shut these eyes
with coins

if you wanted.

Or you could go on
lying about
how the two of us
are indestructible,
how that holy ground
can wait forever

if we wanted.

Let Me Take That Back

Though I swear love,
I do not know
what love is.

A mystery,
an enigma,
a wrapped package
tighter than secrets told
on cold nights,

a hungry wolf
snarling at the moon
rippling on the waters

If Poems Could Save Lives

Wouldn't it be
Beautiful if
Poems could
Save lives,
Race into
Burning houses
And drag out
The victims
Of conflagrations
The way
Our love can?

Valentine's Day

We should smother ourselves
in a mad barrage
of red paper hearts,
red velvet roses

we should lie still as evening
buried beneath
the delightful weight
of our Valentine love

The Rush of Time

It's only time
that escapes us,
those flimsy seconds
racing like flakes
of snow
towards their own
temporal demise.

Only time
that waves
Goodbye
while we stand here
together
in these shared moments.

Only time
wordlessly
deserting us
without once
looking back.

Each Other's Voice

Will we remember
How we measured
Our loneliness
With the yardstick
Of sadness?

Will we recall
How the sound
Of each other's
Voice speaking
Each other's name
Mimicked
The musical strains
Of heaven?

This Time We Have

One more day fell through the cracks.
A thin slice of one more year plunged
like a dagger into the heart of time.
Only fools insist they can prevent
precious moments from slipping away forever.
We have held hands and tried to keep
ourselves rooted in each other's sight.
Color photographs reveal us to the eye
But like most witnesses they tell half-truths.
These prints say we live beyond our numbered years;
The two of us standing there breathlessly still,
Smiles still wide across our faces
as when the photograph froze
us in that joyous moment
But none of that is true. We live and die.
Like workers in a factory,
we add pieces to unfinished puzzles
while the unbeatable clock ticks away.
Still, I would like to speak up about my love
Before the last winds blow words
back down my throat.
I would like to bank on the promises
of faith and vow myself
to you beyond the numbering
of these dying years.

Green

A novice in a world
filled with those
blessed with expertise,
a shade of envy or jealousy,
the color of hard cash
to buy tomorrow's
plastic dreams
or the sweet taste
of spring's
first breath
soft against the bark of
trees awakening.

Painted Lady

Housed on the bark
Of a summer aspen branch,
The lone chrysalis
Delights in the wind's caress
Against its silken self.
Soon the cocoon will tear away:
It is the Law of Nature.
Within its walls
Soon will flutter to life
An untried thing with wings:
A painted lady.

A memory from caterpillar days,
The sun once more will warm her
And the butterfly will hover
Colorful wings
Above the open-petaled faces
Of late-summer flowers.
You see the chrysalis
In the aspen tree? She trembles,
Not in fear but with anticipation.

Somewhere in the garden
She will quench a long thirst
With nectar, she will find a mate,
And pollen speckled on
Her orange wings
She will carry like manna,
Like a lover's kiss,
To the waiting flowers.

Heaven Scent

when you said "Hello, I love you,"
I saw the red sky divide and roses
fall like velvet rain upon my head,
petaled flowers stacking one atop
the other till they made me tall
and proud, and passersby said, "Hey,
that man smells good! He must be glad
to be alive." I tipped my hat.

Fortress

I once believed this heart of mine
in time would prove itself invincible,
that all the armies of life's
discontentment would lay down weapons
and not prevail against me.
Always I boasted a heart of stone, a fortress
where I could be alone to save myself
inside its walls. This faith of mine was strong.
What fool would dare chip away
what I had built! It was a heart
secure within itself, not flesh and blood
like other hearts that pulse away
the fragile time beats of the clock.
Mine was a heart of rock from which
no sound could be heard. Silence
served to put off all who tried
to enter there. Once I believed this heart
could withstand dark sorrows
rapping bloody knuckles against the stone,
but I was wrong. Death danced hypnotic
circles; dizzyingly, I let go.
I lost my faith in what a heart should
and should not be. Have you ever watched
a sculptor work his tools? How gently
he taps away the formless? How patiently?
At my feet you see the graveled stones.
Each one with a name, a life
that once with tender heart unraveled
its moments, ticktocking a life spent

loving others. You see the stones
at my feet? These tears? You hear this heart
now flesh and blood? It is the heart
of a convert, pardoned of all heresy,
beating far from dark and stone.

In the Old Days Poets Took Delight

In the old days poets took delight
in writing poems about their wives.
They were not ashamed to admit
love sat well in lines of romantic verse.
Inked quill in hand they scratched out rhymes.
It was a different time, I know.
Men dressed in buckled shoes, silk cravats,
long white hose women wear today,
and they donned powdered wigs, wore make-up
too! Can you believe what men were back then?
Why, I even read somewhere men would
sit around the house in Sunday clothes!

Not like today where men are men, not
pantywaists with their white handkerchiefs
pulled out of the cuffs of waistcoats to
dab their powdered noses. Heaven forbid!
Today men sit before their TV
sets in their underwear, drinking beer,
or they speed down parkways raging
against other drivers, flipping them off,
swearing as if curses were weapons
and weaving in and out of cars was smart.
Not like today where men wouldn't dream
of lavishing their wives with compliments.

It was different in those days gone by.
Shelly, Keats and Byron before
a fireplace writing poems to
the women they loved. Were they

afraid someone would say, "Pansy!
What's with this sentimental stuff?
Get real. Be a man. Write rough and tough."
They would've laughed. Why, the night Shelley
drowned in a storm at sea he was probably
drunk on Italian wine and poetry!
I'll bet as the water took his life,
in his last breath, he was mouthing
bubbled odes to Mary, love verses.

Poets in the past were unafraid
to write poetry to their wives.
There was no shame attached, no stigma
that would single them out for ridicule.
Today poets write anti-verse
against society, God, the church,
whatever they can sink their claws.
But I would like to stand this moment
in the company of those romantic poets
no longer publishing today:
all those laureates resting somewhere
on their laurels, maybe still writing

love poems to their loved ones.
I would like to step away from poets today
who riddle their poetic lines with
profanity, rough-edged and angry,
heavy as hammers, sharp as nails.
I would like to imitate my
poet-heroes of the past and
say to you, Sharon my love,
in all honesty, these final lines
I write for you at the risk of
sounding love struck, a poet lost

in time: You are the world to me!
In every poem I write your heart
with mine beats between the lines.

Last Night

we lay in bed
on the last night
of the 20th Century
holding hands
whispering prayers
waiting for sleep
to smuggle us
like aliens
past customs
across nightfall

A Heart

Ergonomically speaking, a heart is ill-designed.
Instead of steel or stone or even bone,
a sponge of flesh pumps blood
through arteries and veins.

And it's not round like a ball to roll away
when grief or unrequited love demands
we distance parts of ourselves
in order to survive.

For all its strength and power, the way it marks
the hours without rest, this heart no larger
than a fist, is small enough to rest
encaged within the ribs.

Still, for all the faults we find in its divine
construction, (Engineers surely would have
built it differently), don't we marvel
that a fragile heart reaffirms life,

refusing to succumb to the melancholic
urgings of the brain; that this heart
goes on beating with a kind of courage
inside the husks of last straw.

Eros

They saw him in his angel wings
Bow strung and at the ready
Prowling for prospective lovers

He will take aim and pierce hearts
melt away coldness, make them needy,
And not fly away till they surrender

Eros will bring them up (and down)
on whatever happy (sad) day moves him
But his wounds need not be fatal

The Timekeeper

In our moments the timekeeper
ticked away the time of our lives.
In a slow hand he hurled us
from minute to minute, rag doll heads
stuffed with cotton, our button eyes
dark and blind.

What do we know, we innocents!
Life is a road we travel on.
The sun rises at dawn, sets at dusk,
and we judge passing time by light
and dark. What do we know or
care of clocks!

Remember how we ached to leave
our youth? How the future, a bright
beacon, winked its eye and lured us
into its light? We were both warned:
"Enjoy childhood. Don't grow up so fast.
Life is tough."

Look at us now. Can we admit
Our foolishness? Back then is gone.
Sometimes the laughter we recall
makes us weep. Though the clock ticks its pace,
we pretend it's our fate to live
forever.

The truth beats inside us like drums;
it scares us more than nightmares do:

Time one day will be kept from us.
And we will learn to live somewhere else.

In that clockless silence you and I
will celebrate eternal dawn.

Wake-up Call

when the cats sleep, the world could end;
not even thunder rouses them
nor the loud Latino beat blasting
against our backyard window
nor the screams of summer children.

when the cats sleep, Sharon noiselessly
takes from the kitchen cupboard
a Friskies cat food dinner can.
Cu-Cu slits open golden eyes;
Sperry perks up calico ears,

both wide awake now, racing off
to feast on the specialty of the day:
shredded salmon and fresh water.

Night Visitor

If the Angel of Death suddenly came for you,
I'd trip him down a flight of stairs,
speak defiantly in a voice
sure of life and death, forbid him
to take you from me.

I'd let the Angel rake back long white hair,
flex black wings, stomp his dark sickle,
and flutter back up the stairwell.
Still, come departure time you two,
arm in arm like lovers, will float away.

I will wish for you to turn around
just once and blow sweet goodbye kisses;
Instead two phantoms will vanish
in an unseen destiny

Midnight

in the shadow of the moon
we lovers give two stars
our names:

"This way we'll live forever!"
I say to you,
My face half in darkness,
My heart bursting with love.

"We'll fly towards the heavens!"
you say to me,
your green eyes dotted with tiny stars,
your lips rich with promises.

On The Last Day

When the world ended, everyone of us
knew exactly where we were, what we were
doing, which words, so rudely interrupted
by death, gurgled in the throat of time

You were calling me to dinner; I was
sitting at the computer, laboring
with an intractable metaphor that vanished
like a mirage on a desert of white sand and sky.

Upstairs Grace the landlady called to her dog,
but Sluggo did not bark nor patter across
the living room floor above us. Outside,
sparrows were struck dumb. The world had ended.

Taken by surprise, we had no time
for memorable last lines or holding hands.
All the plans we made— those joys for which
we never found the time—no longer would haunt us.

What did we expect? A dress rehearsal?
The end to come at the stroke of midnight
closing an old millennium? Sunday
perhaps while we were comfortably at rest?

When it came it tiptoed past the broken clocks,
hushed even the air that swirled in and out
of living things, cloaked the sun in a veil of
dark woe, and caught the two of us rooms apart.

The world knew exactly where it stood
before it fell: the twist of a hand, an eye
half blinking, a still life burned to ashes.
At the screen I struggled with a poem.
From the kitchen a world away I heard you

call my name.

Taking on the World

I'll be lifting up the sky again,
putting the sun and clouds back
where they belong. Tonight the stars
will occupy my leisure time,
those lazy moments when I will strain
with all my strength to bear my shoulders
to the weight and standing straight and tall
propel a volley of planets
into dark suspension. It has been
this way for as long as I remember:

waking up before the light
to deja-vu a groggy self through
creature habits like some actor
in a successful play who says
his lines and at the same time thinks
a string of unfinished business.
Why is it so? Why take the world on?
It saddens me that guarantees
are not forthcoming: I can slip
and fall and crash like crystal.

I can stall the blood rhythms
of this pulsing heart and tumble
somersaulting into abysmal silence.
And what if *you* suddenly woke up
delighted in your newfound loneliness,
free of me, free of these hands
juggling moon and fiery comets,
rid at last of these bruised bones,

these eyes that hold you
clear as afternoon even through
tears streaking
in the wake of your brief absences.

Identity

who I really am inside of me?
a stranger, a double agent
with false names, secret papers,
two masks to save my skin,
a pistol the color of blue-black sky.

who I am underneath this shell?
one who befriends his enemies
who forges their pasted smiles
across their opened throats.
who I am? The real me?

I hardly know him: a man alone
on crowded streets, a garbled voice
on the telephone, a collar turned up
against the wind, a hand without tremors.
eyes deep—ocean-blue, unblinking.

a man in a dark coat and hat
in the company of his own
long shadow both waiting
under a bridge on a rainy night
when no one is safe.

The real me maybe holds his breath,
maybe hides behind the shutters
maybe fears his cover will be blown
and he will have to claim me
like a soul owns up to a body

who am I beneath this armor?
Only your love peels away
thick coats of incognito.

Rhymes

It's no accident
as far as I'm concerned
that "wife" and "life" rhyme.

Now you may insist
I take a look at "knife" and "strife"
and explain their place
since both of them also rhyme.

It's the old story of the glass, I think:
half-empty, half-full.
I prefer the full glass of sparkling drink.

These Eyes

Every image is a miracle,
a technicolor explosion of things
that scurry on their way to or back
from their appointments,
even the leaves of autumn
rushing to their brittle deaths
beneath the sneakered feet
of Saturday little leaguers
late for the big game.

Everything these eyes can capture
is a miracle: ace dragonflies
in play, crumpled litter
scuttling up and down the concrete walk.
These eyes that look at you
smiling away grief and sorrow.
These eyes that memorize the turn
of your face, the way you walk,
the shadows you toss as you enter
and exit the moments of my life.

Two's a Couple

Petrarch had his Laura,
Dante, Beatrice.
Browning loved Elizabeth,
So how about a kiss?

Shakespeare loved the theater,
Barrymore, his booze.
John Booth's last performance
Got very bad reviews.

Nixon had his Watergate,
Clinton smoked cigars.
Carter had his liver pills,
Jack loved movie stars.

Some bugs live in soil,
Some inside a rug.
Some are quite annoying.
So how about a hug?

Poets spend their free time
Writing lines of bliss.
I'm not writing at this moment,
So how about a kiss?

The Me Singing Rock 'n Roll

The me you saw yesterday
the me you heard singing off key
in the morning shower
the me singing rock 'n roll
from the fabulous fifties

The me who once carried
a lucky Ace comb
for the dark pompadour I wore
like Jimmy Clanton whom
you say you never heard of

The me you claim never talks
in my sleep
the me who wore a coat
of black leather
the me who still looks for my father
down dark lonely streets

the me who catalogs dreams
of fat and lean years
the me on the furry backs
of runaway squirrels

The me leaning over
the Arno River Bridge
the me in a sun ray
in the crack of a door
clumsily groping for time

The me making faces
in distorted funhouse mirrors
in Sunday morning puddles
in the windows of strangers
in magic lamps rubbed the wrong way

The me you saw chasing the shadows
Of skyscrapers high as the moonlight.
The me of the now and before
the me of never again
The me and the me and
The me you saw touching

The granite of graves
the me peeling moments
like dead layers of skin
the me who I am, who I've been,
will one day become

The me you say totters
like a weathervane rooster
flapping my arms as if I had wings
the me on the roof slant
reaching for heaven
the me on the roof slant
loved by an angel.

That First Afternoon

Summer was when we found each other.
A hot late summer found the two of us
new to each moment we shared as
Debbie drove her little red car.
Every moment drove home God's plan.
We listened to her, kept our attention
on all she said. Our hands distanced between us
made us so far strangers, but then
I took your hand and knew
I would hold that hand forever.

I Am Not the Captain

When the ship goes down
and the captain forgets
his sailor's oath, rows
away on a hidden raft,

I will stand my ground:
forever your hero true as
cool water to tongues
wagging at mirages,

your hero dogged like
the long dark strides of night
snapping at the purple heels
of morning.

Table Poem

I am sending my love
From a moment
That's passing

I'm sending it to you
On the face of a napkin
A moment from now

It's a note at the table
Take it and keep it
Keep it forever

And know mine's a love
Unfettered by time

The Sun

What would the sun say
If he could speak a language
Beyond the garbled words
Of gushing fire?

Would he, true to form,
Say kind words
To warm the coldest hearts?

On the Sea

Despite the passage
Of our time together,
I am still amazed
That on this sea of love
I am standing on the deck
Beside the one
Who healed me
Of my fear of
impending

Loneliness.

In the Silence

The moon is shining down
celestial secrets,
those heavenly tidbits
overheard in the dark silence
of dark night.

She is whispering
from so far away
all we need to know,
and we on this October evening
stand in this square of moonlight,

our hands upturned
like children waiting to catch
white flakes
to daub their palms,
each one a falling star,

a miracle in miniature,
a light touch
of white star dust.

The Way They Do in Spring

Late October says the leaves are dying,
Denuding trees shiver as if in shame,
Blotches of blue pinch their way
Through apertures in overlapping branches,
the moon dreads the advent of
The cold gray sky. But you and I
Celebrate the way they do in spring:

We cheer new life, applaud the manner
In which our love goes on sprouting
Green wings despite the sallow face
Of Mother Nature knitting woolen gloves
as she rocks in her chair
wheezing last labored breaths of autumn.

When the World Stops

On the treadmill of the everyday,
we glide through the motions
as if to take our leisure
would upset life's equilibrium.

We need to make believe
the world stops now and then,
freezes in its cycles,
quits spinning long enough

for us in our stillness
to devour each other with our eyes,
say mutely again and again
how deeply we love each other.

Time Like Sand

Listen to the clock
blow its seconds away
like castaways
of sand grains
dispossessed
from the comfort
of the beach.

Words Say What?

I want to tell everything
that breathes and does not breathe—
people, wildlife,
flames, pebbles, the wind—
tell all creation

how much I love you
but I cannot coax the words
from deep inside me.
Each time I try, I fail.
Love cannot be expressed

in words. Poets have failed
as well, though words
are their tools of trade.
These countless words
I have rehearsed in my poetry,

all arranged in the softness
of poetic lines,
words to dance across the page,
words to reach out
in a lover's embrace,

words that imitate the songs
of birds, words that sparkle
like precious stones,
words culled from the bottom
of my heart, words of devotion

and respect, of undying love—
all these words mere shadows
of my deepest timid self,
reflections of what I wish
I could say to my beloved

but the words stumble
on their lines, they choke
in my throat, they sputter,
spill, leave me sad in the company
of profound silence.

The Stars

The heavens are populated
with innumerable stars
we see as far-off flecks,
even the ones light years
away that burned out
and died when Earth
was very young.

We marvel at how those stars
in their celestial formations
decorate the night skies
with muraled specks of
radiance, how so many
together outline
panoramically

mythological beasts
and beast slayers
reminding us each night
how the world is
both good and evil,
how in a twinkling
we can decide to do battle

with our demons or forget heroes,
become demons ourselves.
We can either look up
and be inspired or find cause
to distrust a dark Heaven.

Will the Ink Run?

Who will read these little journals
when the two of us are gone?
Will the ink run? The pages discolor?
Will someone read them
and pass them on so more will know
the two of us for a little while
lived here and loved here,
and delighted in each other's dreams?

My Pen

I envy my pen
that so effortlessly
declares love.
If only I had its voice!
If only I were so brave!
Look how it transforms
a page of silence
into an aria
of undying song.

Storm

Hot-wiring the horizon,
Lightning accelerates skittish clouds
In a breakneck, thundering frenzy
While twin suns on tangerine fire
Crackle in our eyes.

Holding hands on the sofa, we watch
The late-afternoon sky show
Through our backyard window,
Electro-etching one more
Memory in the making.

When I look back at you again,
You are still there.

The Tiny Moon

under a ganglia of burnt-umber branches
shadows grotesquely twist and hide themselves
on the grayery in evening gardens

but not for long. Already the sun ascends,
bursting at the pencil-lined horizon,
while morning clouds, feigning soft purity,

challenge the new sky, imperceptively
scumbling the rough edges of midnight blue.

the two of us, meanwhile, lie in bed:
you asleep, I free of dreams' entanglements.

on your wrist, glowing like a tiny indiglo moon,
time ticks the seconds slowly away.
on the pillow your face— how peaceful!
on the pillow like strands of gold filigree
your hair.

True Love

in years to come when life
has been all it's meant to be
and songs once sung are stilled

then angels pure and white
as star flakes in earthly winter
sing "You're Home at Last,"

you and I who lived
our lives in love
will come to know at last

the love we shared together
was true love all along.

Daily Offering

These words I offer you
like sacrificial lambs
on the altar of love
do not hint of dying
but of life. From the safe
house of the inner me
words heave against silence
until I'm overwhelmed
and saying "I love you"
becomes the highest praise
the most sacrosanct of prayers
a confession from one
who admits no words have
yet been penned to pronounce
what a sacrament love is
or say without you
how this fool could survive
the absence of your grace.

Rendezvous

A herd of sleep gnomes
trampled across
my closed eyelids
so I followed
the crackling thunder
to the opaque forest
where you were shivering
in the silver rain,
your back pressed
against the trunk
of a plywood tree.

Not This Year

There will be no
Valentine candy
this year.

For sweetness
we will snack
on the bonbons
of shared joys,

munch on
the chocolates
of our contentment,

and we will save
our teeth, grow thin,
fattened on
our love.

When These Wings Envelop Us

The war in Iraq
Still rages
Like demons
Loosened
On the world.
Still, our love
Is at peace;
Its wings
Flutter softly
Like those
Of angels.
When these wings
envelop us,
We rest
within their warmth.

Coins of Joy or Sorrow

When day burns away at sundown
to a smoldering of ash,
the insistent wind carries it away;
all the used-up seconds powdering
in a heap of memory
are swept away into the history
of limitless sky.

In the morning new time raises
its proud head and marches forward
in the shadow of the sun.
This new day will fill the pockets
with coins of joy or sorrow;
it will speak loving endearments
or spew insults and injustices
to all who greet it.

Let us reach out to this new day,
the two of us together.
Let us fill its hands and head with gifts
to take into memory.
Let us whisper of love and forever
so that when night sets day afire
with the sun's last power,

it will not burn to ash and dust
and somehow it will remember
what we vowed, how we loved
each other, and let the words
we spoke be the last words
day whispers to the expanse
of wind and sky.

The Treasure of Love

Who ever said
love was easy?
Who was that wise man
opening up that treasure chest
and sighing
at the beads of color,
the pirate silver,
the blinding slices
of little suns?

The Charity of God

When the summer once hot and sweltering
cooled into autumn and trees once so proud
lost leaves and dreaded wooded nakedness

When fall came and bore the brunt of heavy
feet crunching brittle leaves in their walkings
when shivering colors bundled in a coat of white

when hope wriggled under stones and seeds slept
animals instinctually dreamed in
white and ice their hibernating nightmares

God ordained that the two of us join hands
and hearts, seal our love in matrimony
when all of this marked our days we knew

how truly awesome is the charity of God

I Don't Say the Words

but to me
you are most
beautiful.

The inner me
The outer me
live for your
laughter.

Three More Poems for Sharon

i

My poems to you
are my favorite attempts
at saying what and who
    I am.

And I am not ashamed
if they cannot fly
or if they totter
when I walk them
on the page.

they are my only defense
against what you
might wonder about
    my love.

They are soldiers
in the war against
terrors of the heart.

ii

Looking in my wedding band,
I see not only my face
In its golden reflection
But yours as well.
It is a ring of magic,
Worth more than the gold
Of kings,
More golden than the sun.

When I spin it
Around my finger
The world is beautiful.

    iii

The last word
has not been said.
When that last word comes,
it will float light and airy,
like a love bird's feather.

It will dance in
life's final moments.
It will trip off these feeble lips
like a spring's parting breeze.
It will gush from a mouth
weary of speaking:
    "Sharon."
    "Sharon."

Home Security

The terrors have settled down.
We stopped hearing the rhetoric of war.
The tick-tack of artillery fire
has hushed to cricket volume.
All is once more as it was
before a sad September
crushed a nation
in a vise of fear and panic.

The terrors lie low in a thicket of gray.
We hardly see them beyond the pale lights
flickering in their eyes.
We tell ourselves our love is strong
enough to shut the taps, to pull the plug,
to close the windows and the doors,
say no with all our being,
say no to the enemies of love,
say no in the way we live our lives:

In all the kindnesses
we gather to ourselves.
The terrors have settled down.
We are safe in our apartment.
We pray for a forecast
of sunny Septembers.

The Vase's Last Rose

Let's face it, red flower:
summer is not a magic crayon
with which I can slash away
winter, bleed back into her
the colors you so gracefully flaunt.
If I could, I would grasp summer
like a sword, do battle
with the enemies of green,
proclaim winter, even autumn
and spring, in seasonal disfavor.
Through the opacity of the vase,
I see you, Valentine's last rose,
drooped and petal-worn
atop a soft-thorned stem.
If I could, I would wish into my hands
the power to resuscitate the dying,
and you would live in your garden,
not crushed in the pages of a book
but tall and thriving forever.

Courage (a Double Tetractys)

Hearts
Tremble
Fearlessly
Love can do that
See the leaves flutter in early springtime

Who argues they tremble, fearing winter
Hearts are like that
Love beckons
And they
Beat

To a Woman Worthy of Love

i

What is it about poets that they save
love words for paper, let sentiment glide
from line to line in loops and flourishes,
but cannot speak them to the lover's ear,
tongue-tied, wordless, dumb to speaking out
exactly what love means?

ii

It's not too late. We can still make love grow
stronger. We can still feed it food of the gods,
nectar from the streams of our daily sailings.
It's not too late to dream the breathless kiss.

iii

Once I was foolish, a man who wore pride
like a new suit and I believed love was
a cosmic joke God laughed when He allowed
hearts to break, but I've been humbled
by our love. Believe me when I say,
Sharon, Love is how I define Forever.

Waiting for Day

The October sky wants us to surmise
What day will bring when the sun comes shining.
It's a game skies play to keep themselves from
Getting bored after they have counted clouds
And the countless stars that blink, then fade
With the first hints of dawn's early sunlight.

In its vast expanse of rippling pink or
Shades of baby blue, the October sky
Hopes we'll play along: What will this day bring?
What joy? What sharp cutting edge of sorrow?
This sky is close enough to Heaven to
Eavesdrop knowledge of hidden things to come.

Sometimes it tells the moon, sometimes the clouds,
Or stars tumbling golden dust towards the Earth.
The October sky divines tomorrow
With its impatient hours waiting in
the wings, and asks in a voice serene-blue
if we would play along, guess the new day.

Eyes skyward, you and I just shake our heads
In our refusal. We will not play that
morning game. We know for sure life is good.
Our love strengthens us in all endeavors,
And so we accept what will come will come.
Then the risen sun floods the October sky

With enough light for that sky to busy
Itself counting clouds in morning roll-call.

The Old Days Are Behind Us

We're in the 21st Century now.
The old days are far behind us
where our mistakes are buried
in the old junkyards there
and the wrong moves we made
we've twisted back in shape
so they are straight
as the canes of blind men,
tapping the rhythm of passing time.

The Children of October

We are the children of October
Who delight in long walks
In the park where bare trees
Line our path, where breezes
Scoot the brittle leaves into the air
Like a skittish gaggle of geese

You and I are October's children
Who once sought comfort in the arms
Of other seasons but found them wanting
Finally we abandoned those broken-down drams
And embraced October of the falling leaves,
The spooky pale moon,
The chill in the spirit-laden air.

I've Told You Without Speaking

I've told you again what I feel.
I've told you again
Like a man raising against
The next moment, raising
to catch up with himself later on.

I've told you without speaking;
I've said words down on paper
where they line up like soldiers
or dancers to music
that drives them to dancing
or they hold hands in each line
Of deep-rooted verse.

I've told you again
in the white noise of silence
how my life has no meaning
when we're not together
and all of these poems
are street-corner beggars
unless they're permitted
to sing praises of you.

Every Lover's Dream

If only
we could
turn the tide
of time
rushing
on its way
to places
we cannot go again,
lure back
those precious hours
we thought
were ours to keep!

About the Author

Sal Amico M. Buttaci is the former editor of *New Worlds Unlimited* and of *Poetidings*, the newsletter of the New Jersey Poetry Society, Inc. His poems, stories, letters, and articles have appeared in *The New York Times, The Record, The New York News, The Writer, Cats Magazine, Christian Science Monitor,* and many other publications here and abroad. He is a long-standing member of the New Jersey Poetry Society, Inc. and writes a column called "Poet Craft" for *Poetidings.*

Buttaci is the author of several books, including *Promising the Moon; A Family of Sicilians: Stories and Poems; Greatest Hits: 1970 to 2000* (Pudding House Press*);* and *Two Can Play This Game: The Saturday Afternoon Poets,* which he co-wrote with poet Paul Juszcyk. He is also the author of a recent chapbook, *Sun Sparks the Day: Poems of Sicily.*

He has conducted hundreds of poetry readings and workshops, most of them in New Jersey libraries, schools, coffeehouses, and on local cable TV. He has also lectured on "Growing Up Sicilian."

Sal Amico M. Buttaci is a reading and writing teacher at a local middle school, as well as an instructor at a local community college. He lives in Lodi, New Jersey, with his wife and soul mate Sharon.